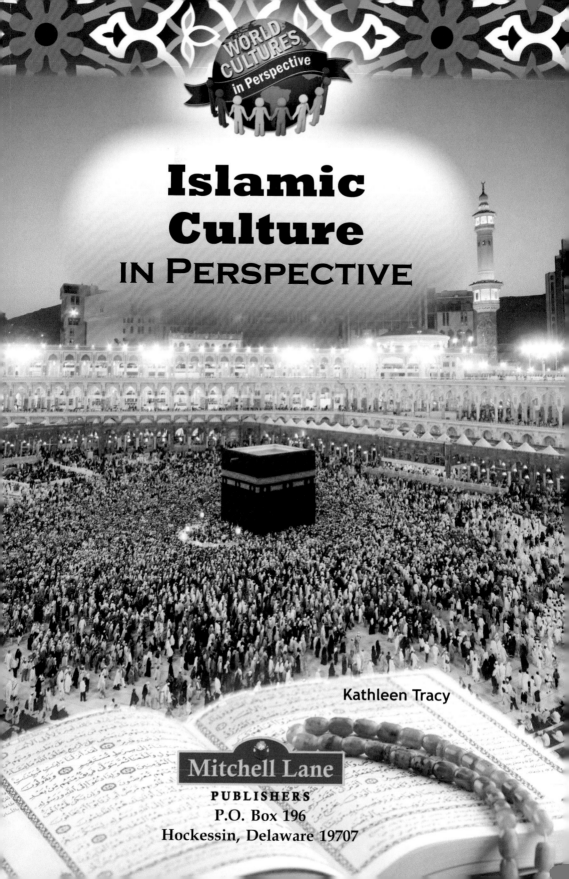

WORLD CULTURES in Perspective

Islamic Culture
IN PERSPECTIVE

Kathleen Tracy

Mitchell Lane
PUBLISHERS
P.O. Box 196
Hockessin, Delaware 19707

WORLD
CULTURES
in Perspective

Brazilian Cultures IN PERSPECTIVE

Caribbean Cultures IN PERSPECTIVE

East Asian Cultures IN PERSPECTIVE

Islamic Culture IN PERSPECTIVE

Israeli Culture IN PERSPECTIVE

Louisiana Cajun & Creole Cultures
IN PERSPECTIVE

Native Alaskan Cultures IN PERSPECTIVE

North African Cultures IN PERSPECTIVE

Polynesian Cultures IN PERSPECTIVE

Southeast Asian Cultures IN PERSPECTIVE

Mitchell Lane
PUBLISHERS

Printing   1   2   3   4   5   6   7   8   9

Library of Congress Cataloging-in-Publication Data
Tracy, Kathleen.
  Islamic culture in perspective / By Kathleen Tracy.
      pages cm. — (World cultures in perspective)
  Includes bibliographical references and index.
  ISBN 978-1-61228-567-2 (library bound)
  1. Islamic civilization—Juvenile literature. I. Title.
  DS35.62.T73 2015
  306.6'97—dc23

                                                        2014009362

eBook ISBN: 9781612286068

PUBLISHER'S NOTE: This story is based on the author's extensive research, which she believes to be accurate. Documentation of this research is on pages 60–61.

The Internet sites referenced herein were active as of the publication date. Due to the fleeting nature of some web sites, we cannot guarantee they will all be active when you are reading this book.

To reflect current usage, we have chosen to use the secular era designations BCE ("before the common era") and CE ("of the common era") instead of the traditional designations BC ("before Christ") and AD (*anno Domini,* "in the year of the Lord").

PBP

CONTENTS

INTRODUCTION
An Ancient Culture in Modern Times

The Middle East is the birthplace of human civilization and a region torn by near-continual tribal wars for thousands of years. It is the inspiration for magical legends and the site of archaeological treasures. It is also home to a variety of religions but is dominated by one of the youngest faiths—Islam. Although the region is generally viewed as the center of Islamic culture, only 18 percent of the world's estimated 1.6 billion Muslims live in the Middle East. Islam is a global religion and its culture is embraced by believers of many races, nationalities, and ethnicities. This book, however, will focus on the cultures of Muslims in the Middle East, where Islam was formed.

A follower of Islam is called a Muslim, which means "one who submits to the will of God." There are five tenets of the faith that Muslims must adhere to: profess there is no god but Allah, and Muhammad is his prophet; pray five times a day while facing the city of Mecca; give to the poor; fast during the month of Ramadan every year; and make a pilgrimage to Mecca once in their life.

Just as Christians and Jews study the Bible and the Torah, Muslims study a holy book called the Quran (also spelled Koran). The teachings of the Quran and the example set by Muhammad during his life form the basis for Sharia (SHah-ree-ah), which is the moral code of Islam. Some conservative Islamic countries are ruled by Sharia law, which is interpreted by Muslim judges. Other countries may apply Sharia only in certain cases like marriage and divorce. While Sharia calls for fairness for all under the rule of law, it is also associated with harsh punishments such as stoning some types of criminals or executing former Muslims who have converted to another religion.

As a result, for people who live in democracies or democratic republics, Islamic culture can seem like a throwback to an earlier, less enlightened era. Western cultures generally share a similar standard of human and civil rights based on secular law going back thousands of years. Elected officials usually run Western governments. Over the past couple of centuries, civil rights have grown in Western countries. In most places in the West, women are no longer considered property and men can no longer abuse their spouses, siblings, or children at will in the name of discipline. Freedom of speech is often taken for granted in the West today. This right is spelled out in a 1948 United Nations document

called *The Universal Declaration of Human Rights*, which many countries later used to form their own laws and policies.

To Muslims in the Middle East, religion is more than a personal spiritual belief and moral compass. While some Middle Eastern nations such as Turkey are secular states, others including Iraq give Islam the status of national religion. Other countries, like Iran and Saudi Arabia, create their laws from the teachings of the Quran. In those nations where there is no separation of religion and state, the nationality of the people is deeply intertwined with their religion.

There are different sects or branches of Islam, some less conservative and others more so. The vast majority of Muslims believe in peace and respecting people of other faiths. *Islam*, after all, is derived from the Arabic word for peace.

However, a minority of so-called radical Islamists believe that terrorism is a justifiable and necessary tool to eliminate non-Muslim cultures. They hope to see the world ruled under their vision of Sharia law. While this group of extremists may be in the minority, they get most of the media coverage, making Islamic culture as a whole much maligned, frequently feared, and generally misunderstood.

The Quran

Written in Arabic, the Quran contains the revelations given to the prophet Muhammad over a period of twenty-two years. The Quran details Islamic laws and commandments that cover the gamut of social and moral behavior. It has five main categories: the nature of the spiritual world; the law and commandments; historical accounts; the wisdom; and the prophecies.

The text of the Quran has remained unchanged down to the last word for the past 1,400 years. The Quran has been translated into more than one hundred languages to help non-believers and even other Muslims to understand the text better. Followers are warned, though, that translations often do not convey the actual meaning and intent of what was revealed. So Muslims are still taught to learn and recite the Quran's passages in Arabic, regardless of what their native language is and even if they cannot understand Arabic well enough to speak it otherwise.

CHAPTER ONE
The Conquest of Mecca

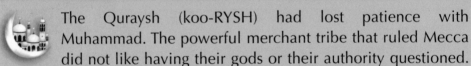

The Quraysh (koo-RYSH) had lost patience with Muhammad. The powerful merchant tribe that ruled Mecca did not like having their gods or their authority questioned. At the time Mecca was a relatively tolerant society where different religions coexisted. Jews and Christians lived alongside those who worshipped many gods. But now Muhammad was openly urging the Quraysh to forsake their idols and accept Allah—or face retribution. Not only were city leaders worried about religious tensions, they were also concerned that Muhammad's public preaching might negatively affect the annual pagan pilgrimage that brought thousands of visitors, and their money, to Mecca.

The tribes of the Arabian Peninsula seemed to be in constant war with one another. But once a year they all called a truce and traveled to Mecca where they would pay homage to the Kaaba, which was used as a temple to house Arabian gods. The famous Black Stone was also inside the Kaaba and visitors would pray before it. The actual structure of the Kaaba was rebuilt several times over the last two thousand years. Today only Muslims can enter Mecca and visit the Kaaba.

Arabs didn't just make the journey in order to honor their gods in the Kaaba. The annual pilgrimage also provided Arabs with an opportunity to work out tribal disputes peacefully, resolve debts, and make alliances. It also allowed them to engage in trade with

Also called the Sacred House, the Kaaba is a cube-shaped building located in the center of Islam's most sacred mosque, Al-Masjid al-Haram, in Mecca, Saudi Arabia. The black cloth covering the Kaaba is called a kiswah and is embroidered with verses from the Quran.

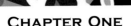
Meccan merchants. So when bribery and threats failed to silence Muhammad, the city leaders resorted to persecution.[1]

After the death of Muhammad's uncle and protector, Abu Talib, his other family members withdrew their protection, putting his life in danger. Around that time, warring factions in Medina—then called Yathrib—asked Muhammad to come and act as a mediator. While there he established an agreement between the groups living in the oasis town. The Charter of Medina would become the foundation for an Islamic state.[2]

In 622 CE, after nearly a decade of conflict with the Quraysh, Muhammad relocated to Medina. That migration became known as the *Hijra*. Once in Medina, the vision of a Muslim community, or *umma*, became a reality. Instead of constructing a community based on family relationships, the community's common belief in Islam became its binding ties. The intent wasn't just to pursue a personal religious belief but to establish Islam as a complete way of life. In Medina, Muslims were able to grow as a community and secure a base from which they would spread Islam across the Arabian Peninsula.

This did not go unnoticed by the Quraysh and tensions continued to simmer. Eventually, the Battle of Badr erupted, and the Muslims defeated the Quraysh army outside Medina. Depending on which historian you believe, the victory was either due to Allah's intervention or Muhammad's deft leadership. What isn't disputed is that the victory only led to a temporary, uneasy peace.

The next battle took place in 625 at Mount Uhud, located about four miles north of Medina. The two sides fought to a draw, with the Muslims and the Quraysh suffering heavy casualties. Two years later at the Battle of the Trench, the Muslims successfully fended off a two-week siege by Arab and Jewish tribes.

In 628, Muhammad and 1,400 Muslims marched to Mecca intending to take part in the annual pilgrimage. Initially, the Quraysh blocked their entry. Instead of creating conflict, the Muslims camped peacefully outside the city. Muhammad and a Meccan official agreed to work out a diplomatic solution and entered into the Treaty of Hudaybiyyah (hooh-day-BEE-yah). The

Quraysh agreed to a ten-year period of peace and promised to admit Muslims into the city to perform the next year's pilgrimage.

Two years later, however, the Quraysh violated the truce when they killed a group of Muhammad's allies. Muhammad led ten thousand Muslim and allied soldiers to Mecca in late 630. He sent four columns of troops into the city, where only one met any resistance. After a brief skirmish, Mecca surrendered. Muhammad granted peace and amnesty to the inhabitants but destroyed their pagan idols and encouraged them to convert. Muhammad declared Mecca as the holiest site in Islam and established it as the center of Muslim pilgrimage.

Muhammad died in 632. In just twenty years since his first reported revelation, he had established a new religion and united Arab tribes into an Islamic culture. Although Muslims revere Muhammad as the prophet and as a role model of faith and piety, they do not worship him. Unlike Jesus, who Christians believe is the son of God and therefore divine, Muhammad has always been perceived as very much human—just an extraordinary human.

Al-Masjid al-Nabawi, or the Prophet's Mosque, was built by Muhammad in 622 near his residence in Medina.

A Muslim student at the Hebrew University of Jerusalem in Israel protests a 2009 campus appearance by *Jyllands-Posten* editor Flemming Rose.

Depictions of Muhammad

In September 2005 the Danish newspaper *Jyllands-Posten* published twelve satirical drawings depicting Muhammad. The newspaper's culture editor Flemming Rose explained, "I commissioned the cartoons in response to several incidents of self-censorship in Europe caused by widening fears and feelings of intimidation in dealing with issues related to Islam."[3]

The cartoons ignited a furious reaction from Muslims the world over because any image of Muhammad is considered offensive, regardless of the context.

Imam Talal Eid explains that Muhammad "instructed his companions not to draw a picture of him, and this has been taken as a general prohibition. He also told them not to pray in places that have images. There also is a general prohibition against full statues."[4]

Other Islamic scholars say the primary reason for the ban on depicting Muhammad is the concern that Muslims might start to worship his image. Political scientist As'ad AbuKhalil notes, "In the Holy [Quran] of Islam, the one sin unforgivable is that of polytheism. The prohibition is intended to protect the faithful from that sin. The fear was that intense reverence for the prophet might if unrestrained cross over into worship. In the eighth and the ninth centuries a general consensus banning such depictions arose among the clerics, but not all Muslims knew of it, paid attention, or obeyed."[5]

That is why there were numerous illustrations of Muhammad drawn by devout Muslims during medieval times. But such art was mostly created for the upper classes that could afford to hire painters.

The modern prohibition has expanded beyond keeping Muslims from worshipping the likeness of Muhammad, as the Danish cartoon controversy shows. Professor of Islamic Studies John Esposito says, "To criticize the prophet Muhammad is as direct an attack as mocking or attacking the [Quran], which is seen as the word of God or the sacred Scripture."[6]

It's not just images of Muhammad that are considered offensive; many Muslims believe that all drawings and paintings of living creatures are prohibited. There is one exception to the prohibition against images and statues: children are allowed to play with dolls because there's no fear that they will worship them as idols.

CHAPTER TWO
Evolution of Islamic Culture

 Muslims call the time prior to Muhammad the Age of Ignorance. Before the emergence of Christianity and Islam, Arabs believed in many deities, just as the Romans and Greeks did. Three of the best-known were goddesses. Manat was the goddess of destiny; Allat was the motherly, nurturing goddess; and Al-Uzza was a love and war goddess. In addition, each tribe worshipped its own particular gods and goddesses. Muhammad's tribe, for example, worshipped a tree goddess called Dhat Anwat at a tree that was found on the road connecting Mecca to Medina. So unlike the Greek gods that united the various Greeks, the early Arab religions varied according to tribe.

But other factors also separated Arabs and by the time of Christ, the northern tribes had developed into two different cultures. The nomadic Arabs were Bedouin shepherds who lived in small tribes that were extremely close-knit. The sedentary Arabs were also Bedouins, but they were involved in trade and chose to settle in the oases that line the edge of the Arabian Desert, along the land trade routes.

Most of these oasis settlements were not established until after 1000 BCE. Whereas the nomadic Arabs were a peaceful people, the sedentary Arabs often found themselves having to use military force to protect the oases' precious resources from invaders. The sedentary Arabs prospered through trade and as a result grew more powerful than their nomadic neighbors.

Bedouins mainly live in the Arabian and Syrian deserts, the Sinai Peninsula of Egypt, and the Sahara Desert of North Africa. They are best known for their once-nomadic lifestyles. But today only approximately 5 percent of Bedouins still live as pastoral nomads. The rest live in or near cities, or in small desert communities, such as this one in Wadi Rum, Jordan.

Over time Christianity and Judaism spread throughout the peninsula. But the religious and cultural landscape of Arabia changed forever in the early seventh century when Muhammad founded Islam.

One night during Ramadan, the traditional Islamic month of spiritual retreat, when Muhammad was about forty years old, the angel Gabriel appeared to him in the form of a man and told him he was the messenger of God. After praying and meditating on the vision, Muhammad accepted the responsibility to spread the message of God.

After Muhammad conquered Mecca, other tribes surrendered to the Muslims. But to be fully secure, the Muslims needed to expand their territory. Muhammad used Islam to unite the different Arab tribes within an Islamic Empire. And at the time of his death in 632 CE, Muhammad controlled a majority of the Arabian Peninsula. Over the next millennium, Islam would become the primary religion of the entire Middle East as well as a way of life for Arabs.

Starting in 633 the Muslim armies fanned out over the Arabian Peninsula, spreading their religion and language rapidly over vast areas of the world including southwestern Asia, Persia, parts of India, Afghanistan, Turkestan, Syria, Palestine, Egypt, North Africa, and Spain.

In 639, for example, the Arabs invaded Egypt, and by 641, they had driven the Romans out of the country (see map below). After being conquered by the Arabs, most Egyptians eventually converted from Christianity to Islam.

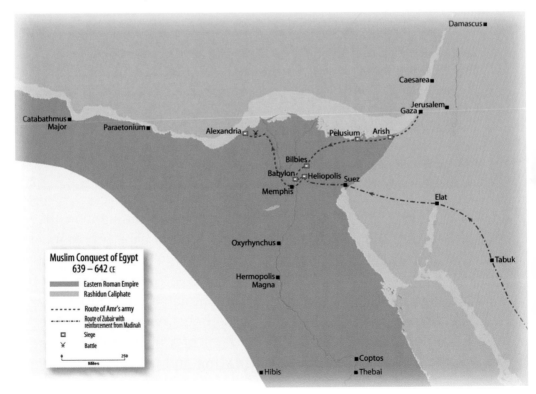

Muslims did not use violence to convert conquered peoples to Islam; they used incentives instead. Once an area was conquered, Islam became the official religion of the land. Because Muslims were not required to pay taxes, most of the new subjects became willing converts. Arabic was widely adopted, eventually becoming the common language of most of the conquered areas.

Pre-Islamic Arabs were a tribal people; they lived in their own groups across the peninsula. Because of this, each tribe had individual customs but there was not a singular Arab culture. As the Islamic empire grew, Muslims expanded their knowledge through exposure to the cultures of the peoples they conquered, particularly the Greeks and Persians.

Islamic civilization entered a golden age in the eighth and ninth centuries, and during that time Greek and Persian traditions were integrated with Arab customs. Muslim scientists studied the theories and discoveries of earlier scientists in Alexandria, Egypt, and scholars rediscovered ancient Greek science and philosophy through their contact with the Byzantine Greeks. The culture of the Byzantines was itself a combination of the Christian religion, Greek culture, and Roman government. Muslims are credited with reintroducing the Greeks' mathematical and scientific contributions to Medieval Europe, which had been lost during the Dark Ages.

Muslim philosopher Averroes lived in the twelfth century. He translated the works of Aristotle into Arabic, helping to integrate Aristotle's ideas into Islamic philosophy.

17

Cordova, Spain

The Moors

Long before the arrival of the Islamic Arabs, North Africa was inhabited by native Berbers, whose culture can be traced back for thousands of years. The ancient Romans called the Berbers *Mauri*, or Moors. In the seventh century Muslims conquered the Berbers and converted them to Islam. Europeans continued to call the now-mixed Arab-Berber population Moors.

In 711, the Muslim Moors invaded Spain and eventually conquered most of the Iberian Peninsula. Moorish Spain was most noted for art and education. The Moors introduced many crops such as rice, cotton, sugarcane, and dates; built irrigation systems; and advanced mathematics, medicine, and the physical sciences.

The city of Cordova became a cultural center where the Europeans rediscovered the Greek classics. Cordova was state-of-the-art in its time, with paved streets that were lit at night with a system of lamps. Everyone in Moorish Spain was given an education; the region had seventeen universities and more than seventy public libraries.

The Moors ruled Spain for seven centuries until it was eventually conquered by Christians in the late fifteenth century. The Moors were given the choice to convert to Christianity or leave Spain. Those who converted were called Moriscos, however most retained their customs and secretly remained Muslims.[1]

CHAPTER THREE
Muslim Religious Traditions

One of the most unique traditions in Islamic culture is the Hajj, the yearly pilgrimage to Mecca. According to Islamic law, Muslims must make the pilgrimage at least once in their lifetime, unless they are prevented by a physical disability, or they can't afford to do so.

By taking part in the Hajj, Muslims show their unity and submission to Allah. The pilgrimage begins on the eighth day of Dhul Hijjah, the twelfth month of the Islamic calendar. Hajj is associated with Ibrahim (Abraham), a key figure in both the Old Testament of the Bible and the Quran. Ibrahim is known for his efforts to establish a personal relationship with Allah.

Ibrahim left his home in the city of Ur after challenging the locals' worship of idols, statues, and stones. He settled in Egypt and later had a son, Ismail (Ishmail), with his second wife Hajar (Hagar). Allah commanded Ibrahim to take Ismail and Hajar to Mecca, and to trust that Allah would care for them. Allah responded to Hajar's prayer for water by making a spring appear miraculously. Eventually, passing traders stopped and asked Hajar if they could water their camels. Over time, more and more traders settled by the spring, and the area eventually became the city of Mecca. Ibrahim returned on occasion to visit. The first Hajj took place when Allah commanded Ibrahim to build the Kaaba in Mecca.

Once a year, about three million Muslims gather in Mecca to perform a series of rituals and prayers at both Al-Masjid al-Haram, and locations around Mecca with religious significance, such as Mount Arafat. Al-Masjid al-Haram, which can hold more than eight hundred thousand people, is considered the holiest mosque in the world by Muslims. It contains the cube-shaped Kaaba, which Muslims believe is located at the first place on earth that Allah created for religious worship. When Muslims face Mecca to pray, they are actually facing the Kaaba.

Just as there are various denominations of Christianity, there are different sects of Islam. Globally, an estimated 87 to 90 percent of Muslims belong to the Sunni sect; most of the rest are Shia Muslims. Although they are outnumbered worldwide, Shiites are the majority in Iraq, Iran, Bahrain, and Azerbaijan, and are significant minorities in Yemen, Saudi Arabia, Afghanistan, India, Lebanon, Pakistan, Syria, Turkey, and Kuwait.[1]

The Shia and the Sunni share the same basic beliefs of Islam, just as Baptists and Catholics both believe Jesus was the son of God. But after the death of Muhammad, there was a disagreement over who should take his place as the Muslim leader. A majority of prominent Muslims maintained Muhammad had not named an official successor so they named the prophet's advisor Abu Bakr, as the first successor, or caliph. This upset Muslims who believed that Muhammad had chosen his son-in-law, Ali ibn Abi Talib, to succeed him.

Ali did not actively oppose the election of Abu Bakr. But his supporters believed that direct descendants of Muhammad were the only rightful Muslim leaders. They became known as the Shia, which came from *Shi'at Ali*, or "the party of Ali." Those who believed that Islamic leaders should be chosen based on their ability to be both a secular and religious leader became known as the Sunnis. Ali eventually became the fourth caliph, but his brief reign ended with his assassination and the rift between the two sects continues to this day.

Shiites believe that religious leaders called imams, descendants of Muhammad's family, have the exclusive right to interpret Islamic law. Sunni Muslims argue that leadership is not a birthright, but needs to be earned and can be given or taken away by the Muslim people.

In the centuries after Muhammad died, many foreign invaders competed for control of Arabia. By the early 1500s, the Ottoman Empire, sometimes called the Turkish Empire, had conquered most of the region. In the eighteenth century, the Arabian Peninsula was divided into different principalities. The state of Saudi Arabia began in the central region of Najd near modern-day Riyadh. The local ruler named Muhammad bin Saud partnered with Islamic activist Muhammad bin Abdul-Wahhab to create a new political group based on Islam.

Saud and Wahhab both wanted all Muslims to adhere to Islam in its purest form. In 1744, they made a pact to make that vision a reality, and created the First Saudi State. They further cemented the deal when Saud's son married Wahhab's daughter, binding the two families together.

Wahhabi leaders waged a jihad, or holy war, against other, less strict sects of Islam on the Arabian Peninsula and succeeded in uniting most of Arabia. This alarmed the Turks, who wanted to keep the region peaceful. By 1818, the Wahhabis were driven out of power by the Turks and their Egyptian allies.

In 1902 Abdulaziz al-Saud and his Wahhabi followers captured Riyadh. Over the next three decades he systematically brought more and more of Arabia under his control, and in 1932 he officially established the Kingdom of Saudi Arabia. Arabic was its official language and the Quran was its constitution. Wahhab's version of Islam is the official religion of the state today; other versions of Islam are considered false. The Saud Dynasty remains in power in the country. As the home of Mecca and Medina, Saudi Arabia continues to be an important cultural center for Muslims around the world.

In 1932, after consolidating power throughout the Arabian Peninsula, Abdulaziz al-Saud renamed the area Saudi Arabia. He then proclaimed himself King of Saudi Arabia.

Mosques

The first mosques were built in the seventh century shortly after Muhammad established Islam. More than just places to pray, mosques became symbols of community and closeness to God. When Islamic armies conquered a new region, they established a mosque in the area soon after. In many cases, they simply converted churches into mosques, or built their mosques on sites where churches or temples had once stood. Al-Masjid al-Haram, the largest mosque in the world, was built around the Kaaba shortly after Muhammad's death. It has been modified numerous times in the centuries since.

Officially all Muslims, regardless of sects, are welcome to enter any mosque, but usually Muslims pray at a mosque run by their particular sect even when traveling. Some mosques prohibit non-Muslims from entering, but many mosques are open to everyone. Visitors still need to follow the customs associated with entering a mosque, like wearing modest clothing. Muslims must purify themselves before praying, so fountains or washing stations are located at the entrances. When entering a mosque, everyone must take off their shoes to keep the area clean for prayer. In the majority of mosques, men and women are segregated into their own praying areas.

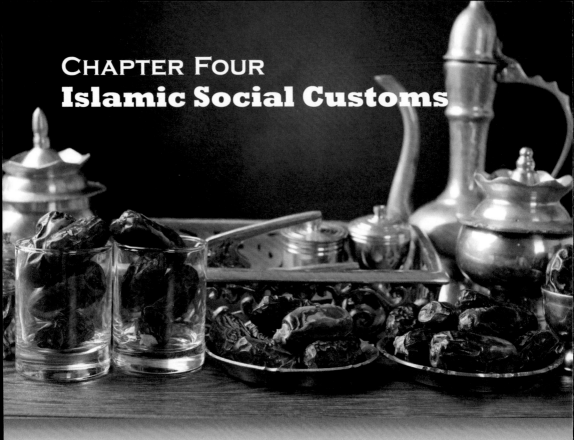

CHAPTER FOUR
Islamic Social Customs

Religion informs every aspect of Islamic culture, from politics to social engagement. Muslims around the world have different cultures that are largely influenced by their location. But even within the Middle East, Muslim social customs vary widely.

There are many similarities, however. For example, Muslims are prohibited from drinking alcohol, so you won't find alcohol at most Muslim dinners and social gatherings in the Middle East. In some countries, like Saudi Arabia and Kuwait, alcohol is not permitted for anyone, Muslim or not. Family meals are a time to relax. Men and women eat together unless unrelated males are present; in those cases women may be segregated. Likewise, at parties, men and women tend to be segregated.

It is common to eat while sitting on the floor in some countries. Muslims will only eat using their right hand because the left hand is considered unclean. While there is a lot of conversation before and after meals, dinner itself is usually eaten in silence so the food can be fully appreciated.

There are also universal Islamic holidays and celebrations that cross national and ethnic boundaries. Eid al-Adha, the Feast of the Sacrifice, is observed at the end of Hajj. In most places, the celebration lasts several days. The exact dates of the Feast vary because Islamic months begin at sunset on the day when the lunar crescent first appears after the new moon, and can be seen with the naked eye. Visibility depends on unpredictable factors such as weather conditions, so Eid al-Adha and other holidays have typically been celebrated on different days in various areas of the world. Also, because Islamic dates are determined by a lunar calendar, the Feast of Sacrifice is observed about eleven days earlier each subsequent year.

The month of Ramadan is a time of personal reflection, spiritual renewal, and strict fasting; eating and drinking are prohibited during the daylight hours of Ramadan, but Muslims are allowed to feast after nightfall. At the end of Ramadan, there is an exuberant celebration called Eid al-Fitr, the Festival of Fast-Breaking.

Before the start of Eid each Muslim family gives a donation of food to the poor, such as rice, barley, and dates. This ensures that even needy Muslims can have a holiday meal and participate in the celebration. The charitable donation is known as Sadaqah al-Fitr, charity of fast-breaking.

Eid al-Fitr falls on the first day of Shawwal, the month that follows Ramadan in the Islamic calendar. In the morning, Muslims gather early in outdoor locations or mosques to perform the Eid prayer, which is a short congregational prayer followed by a sermon. After the sermon is finished, everyone leaves to visit family and friends. It is common to bring gifts, especially to children. The celebration can last as long as three days.

Individual countries also have their own holidays. National Saudi Day is a popular secular holiday in Saudi Arabia. There are many people in the country who believe that only religious holidays should be celebrated. Every year, though, Saudis celebrate by playing music, waving the Saudi flag, and watching fireworks.

In Persian Gulf countries like Kuwait, shopping is a favorite pastime. Locals can often be found haggling over prices in the

Eid al-Fitr is a holiday which marks the end of the Ramadan fast. During Eid al-Fitr, people exchange gifts, and friends and family feast together.

local *souk*, or market, then eating a leisurely lunch or dinner at their favorite restaurants.

In Egypt, Turkey, and other more moderate Muslim countries, women are modestly but fashionably dressed, their heads often covered with colorful scarves. In more conservative countries like Saudi Arabia, however, women are required to wear *burqas*, full-

Middle Eastern souks are the traditional shopping centers of the region. A wide variety of items can be found in souks, like this one in Kuwait.

Women wear different types of clothing across the Middle East. In Saudi Arabia, one of the most conservative countries, women are required to wear burqas like the one this woman is wearing.

body cloaks, and a scarf called the *hijab* that covers the head and hair, leaving only the face or eyes visible.

In most Islamic countries education is highly valued and girls as well as boys can attend school, although they attend separate, same-sex schools. In Saudi Arabia, many women work in professions such as teaching, medicine, and social work, where they may not be required to have contact with men. But more jobs are becoming available to those women who are willing to work alongside men; and more women are considering and accepting these jobs. Still, physical contact between men and women in public is considered inappropriate and offensive in most Islamic Middle Eastern countries.

While many social customs derive directly from either the Quran or the *hadith*—Muhammad's actions or comments—other customs are simply local traditions incorporated into regional Islamic communities. For example, Arabs of the same gender shake hands both when they meet and when they say goodbye.

Marriages also follow a strict protocol. In Islam, marriage is a legal contract as much as a social agreement. Both the bride and groom have to consent to the marriage verbally and in writing. The process begins with a formal proposal of marriage and acceptance of the proposal. For first marriages, the bride is typically represented in the contract negotiations by a male guardian.

The groom presents the woman with a bridal gift, or *mahr*, that becomes her sole property. The mahr can be cash, jewelry, or property, and payment is either due in full when the marriage contract is signed or can be paid in installments.

Two adult witnesses are required to verify the marriage contract. Both parties have the option of including conditions such as where

According to the teachings of Islam, education is very important. However, depending on the country, formal education for girls may be limited or discouraged.

Though she was born in the United States, Sarah Attar also has Saudi Arabian citizenship through her father. In the 2012 Olympics, she became one of the first two women to compete for Saudi Arabia. Attar said, "This is such a huge honor and an amazing experience, just to be representing the women."[1]

they will live, if the wife can continue working—just about anything is allowed as long as the man and woman agree. The final contract is usually signed in front of immediate family and an imam or someone well-versed in Islamic law. So the actual marriage ceremony is typically a matter of minutes.

Although considered a last resort, couples are allowed to divorce. While a man can initiate divorce by stating his desire to do so aloud or in writing, a woman must go to a judge for a divorce if her husband does not agree. It is recommended that there is a three-month separation after the first time the divorce is declared. If there is no reconciliation, then the divorce is finalized, and the woman is free to marry again after an additional three-month waiting period.

There is often confusion as to whether Muslims can have two or more wives at the same time, which is called *polygyny*. (*Polyandry* is having more than one husband and *polygamy* is a more general definition: having two or more wives or husbands at the same time.)

In the pre-Islamic Arab world, men could marry as many wives as they wanted if they had the resources to support them. The Quran limits the number of wives to four to ensure fair treatment. When Islam was founded, constant warfare in the Arab world resulted in a population that included more women than men. Polygyny ensured that every woman could be married under Islamic law and that orphans would be provided for.

Today polygyny butts heads with secular law. In some Islamic nations, polygyny is still relatively common. But in many countries, polygyny is growing increasingly unpopular. In places like Turkey and Azerbaijan it is illegal. Many other Islamic nations have placed legal restrictions on the practice. In some countries, a man must have the permission of the first wife to marry a second wife. A woman can often specify in her marriage contract that her husband cannot have a second wife. Women's rights activists argue that polygyny has great potential to violate a woman's rights, and therefore should be stopped altogether.

Wedding Celebrations

While the Islamic law aspects of marriage are the same for Muslims everywhere, the public wedding celebrations vary widely depending on the country and local traditions. Here are some of the ways different Muslim cultures throw a wedding party.

Pakistan: Marriage festivities include separate preparation ceremonies for the bride and the groom. During these ceremonies, henna is applied to the hands and feet of the bride and groom. Singing and dancing to the sound of percussion instruments is common at these ceremonies. After the contract is signed a lavish dinner feast is served for family and friends, usually at the home of the bride.

United Arab Emirates: To prepare for the wedding, the woman applies various oils and perfumes to her body and hair. Traditionally, only the bride's family can see her for the forty days prior to the wedding. A couple of days before the marriage, the bride's friends decorate her hands and feet with henna.

Pakistan

Egypt

34

Egypt: Following the signing of the contract, the families honk their horns as they drive to the location of the party. At the party, the bride and groom are greeted by a *zaffa*, a line of dancers, drummers, and other musicians. The first drink is called *sharpat*, a rose water juice.

Iran: For the wedding ceremony, a *sofreh* or spread is laid out in front of the couple with various foods and decorations. A cloth made of fine fabric such as satin or silk is placed on the ground, and good-luck symbols are placed on top of it. One symbol is a tray of seven different spices and herbs of various colors, which keeps evil spirits away. A large mirror and two candles face the couple to bring light to their relationship. Eggs and nuts are placed on the cloth to ensure the fertility of the husband and wife. A bowl of coins represents the new couple's future wealth, and a copy of the Quran represents a union that is blessed by Allah. Sweet pastries on the cloth represent a sweet future for the newlyweds. The *aroosi*, the elaborate reception that follows the wedding, lasts for three to seven days. It can take place right after the wedding, or up to a year later.

Palestine

CHAPTER FIVE
Arts and Sciences

 One of the best ways to learn about a culture is by studying what it creates, from art and architecture to scientific advancements and cuisine.

Throughout the Middle East, Muslims eat foods and dishes traditional to their countries. Meals often include meats like beef and lamb, and vegetables like eggplant, tomato, onion, squash, and okra. Dishes are flavored with spices such as cayenne, cumin, nutmeg, and turmeric. A salad called tabbouleh, made of tomatoes, cucumbers, onion, mint, garlic, and a grain called bulgur, can be found across the Middle East. Turkish delight, a sweet candy that originated in Turkey, is available now in places around the world. Other famous Middle Eastern foods include baba ghanoush, hummus, falafel, and pita bread.

Islamic meals are also determined by the Quran's dietary restrictions. Foods that are allowed are called *halal*. Muslims are prohibited from eating pork, animals that die naturally, and blood. Animals must be killed humanely in the name of Allah and meat

Turkish Delight

The Dome of the Rock is the most famous Islamic site in Jerusalem. Completed in 691, the Dome is a shrine constructed over a sacred stone that Muslims believe is the spot where the Prophet Muhammad ascended into heaven.

must be completely drained of blood before it can be cooked and eaten.

Islamic architecture is best known for its use of domes and cupolas, standard features on mosques. Towers called minarets are used to call Muslims to prayer. Residences also have signature features such as courtyards, which provide outdoor spaces that are contained by the buildings. These courtyards cool homes in summer by allowing breezes to flow through. Today, Middle Eastern cities feature large, modern skyscrapers such as the Burj Khalifa in United Arab Emirates. This building isn't just tall; it's the tallest skyscraper in the world, rising to 2,722 feet (830 meters).

Muslim contributions to literature are not as well known outside the Middle East. While Muslim advances in medicine, geography, mathematics, and astronomy were recognized by Europeans, their literature went largely unnoticed because of translation difficulties. Historically, much of Muslim literature was poetry. One of the

The Sheikh Zayed Grand Mosque Center in Abu Dhabi, United Arab Emirates, is the country's cultural and intellectual center. It is named after the late Sheikh Zayed Bin Sultan Al Nahyan, who was the first president of the United Arab Emirates.

most famous examples of Middle Eastern poetry is *Layla and Maj-nun*, a love story from the seventh century. *One Thousand and One Nights*, another well-known work of fiction, is a collection of Middle Eastern stories that was first translated into English in 1706.

Completed in 2010, the Burj Khalifa tower in Dubai, United Arab Emirates, is the tallest man-made structure in the world, rising to 2,722 feet (830 meters).

Islamic culture has a rich history of scientific discoveries and innovations. Muslims believe that by learning about the world around them, they can better appreciate Allah's creations. Because of this, Muslims were responsible for many of the breakthroughs in science and math that we take for granted today. The field of anthropology, or the study of humans, was founded by Persian scholar Abu Raihan Muhammad Al-Beruni. He also made major contributions to physics, astrology, geography, and mathematics. Much of what we understand about the way light travels and how the human eye works was discovered by Ibn al-Haytham. He was born in the city of Basra, which is located in Iraq.

Although the numbers we use today are called Arabic numerals, the system that they were based upon was actually developed in India over thousands of years. It was Persian mathematician Muhammad ibn al-Khawarizmi who introduced Arabic numerals to the West along with a form of mathematics he called *al-jabr*. In the United States, we call this type of math algebra. Al-Khawarizmi described how to find the square root of a number and how to use equations to calculate unknown values.

Muslims also facilitated advances in medicine. Muhammad encouraged his followers to seek medical treatment for their illnesses, stating that "Allah, the Exalted, has let no disease exist without providing for its cure, except for one ailment, namely, old age."[1] As the Islamic influence grew in the Middle Ages, so did the efforts to keep Muslims healthy. But as with all cultures, location, hygiene, economic factors, epidemics, and climate presented challenges. Nomadic Muslims were particularly vulnerable.

Wealthy citizens received better care in general, but medieval Muslim physicians also tried to treat everyone they could. According to Professor of the History of Islamic Science Emilie Savage-Smith, "The medical care in the medieval Islamic lands involved a rich mixture of religions and cultures to be seen in both the physicians and the patients—a coexistence and blending of traditions probably unrivaled in contemporaneous societies. The medical profession in general transcended the barriers of religion, language, and country."[2]

41

Statue of Abu Raihan Muhammad Al-Beruni in Laleh Park, Tehran, Iran

Modern Islamic attitudes tend toward the holistic, with a combination of science and faith used to maintain good health and heal the sick. For example, the fasting period during Ramadan is considered beneficial for both the soul and the body. The accompanying meditation and prayers bring peace, which Muslims believe promotes health.

Scientists are finding that periodic fasting may actually have measurable health benefits. According to Mark Mattson of the National Institute on Aging, fasting may prevent degenerative diseases like Parkinson's and Alzheimer's, and treat others like asthma.[3] Although his studies support the idea that there are medical benefits associated with fasting, more research needs to be done to say for certain.

Other Islamic health practices include:

- Circumcision of male infants or children is encouraged.
- Blood transfusions are acceptable with proper screening.
- Assisted suicide and euthanasia are not permitted.
- Keeping a terminal patient on life support for a long time in a vegetative state is not encouraged.
- Abortion is only permitted in the first four months of pregnancy, or to save the life of the mother.
- Organ transplants are allowed with some restrictions.
- Cloning is not allowed, but genetic engineering is acceptable for the purpose of curing disease.
- Mothers are expected to breastfeed for two years.

Hospitals

Muslims used knowledge they acquired from Greeks and Egyptians to develop their own medical system. Muslims were the first to develop hospitals, called *bimaristans*. These medical facilities employed Jewish, Christian, and Muslim physicians. But in keeping with Islamic tradition, male and female patients were segregated into separate wards. Likewise, different groups of diseases were assigned different locations.

Muslim hospitals were the first to keep regular records of patients and their medical treatment. They also served as centers for medical education, and provided housing for students and staff alike. The hospitals built in medieval Europe were modeled after Arabian hospitals.

Throughout history Muslims have made great contributions to the field of medicine. Today, many Muslims still choose careers in medicine.

CHAPTER SIX
Politics and World View

In any religion, political system, or cause, there can be extremist groups that cast suspicion and distrust on mainstream members that make up the vast majority. Islam is no different. Some Westerners viewed all Muslims as villains after the attacks by the al-Qaeda terrorist group on September 11, 2001.

Within Islam itself there is an ongoing debate about what exactly it means to be Muslim. For example, Shiites allow temporary marriage that lasts for a predetermined period of time, but Sunnis do not permit this arrangement. Wahhabi or Salafi Islam is the only legal version of Islam in Saudi Arabia, and is more conservative than other forms. Some Muslims also study Sufism, which is considered to be the secret inner teachings of Islam. In some cases, Muslims consider their own form of Islam to be the only true form. In their eyes, people practicing other forms are not Muslims at all.

Many Islamic countries became subtly more secular in the latter half of the twentieth century, particularly concerning women's rights. Other nations like Saudi Arabia, though, remained officially committed to Islamic law. Even so, some Muslims accuse the Saudi royal family of corruption. They claim that although Islamic laws are strictly enforced for citizens, the members of the royal family are not held to the same standards. Some even say they disrespect Islam by drinking alcohol and engaging in dishonest practices.

Saudi Arabia has also been criticized by some of its citizens and by people from other Muslim countries for its relationship with the United States; specifically, relying on the United States military to protect the country from possible attacks by Iraq and Iran. During the Gulf War in 1991, when Iraq invaded Kuwait, American and United Nations troops maintained a base camp in Saudi Arabia.

The continued presence of American troops in Saudi Arabia after the Gulf War ended outraged certain Muslims. In particular,

US Army General Norman Schwarzkopf Jr. led the coalition forces during the Gulf War. He says his strategy for 1991's Operation Desert Storm to drive Iraqi troops out of Kuwait was fairly simple. "It's an analysis of your enemy to learn their strengths and weaknesses. You know your strengths and weaknesses, and then you just use your strengths against their weaknesses."[1] Schwarzkopf died in December 2012.

On September 11, 2001, terrorists associated with al-Qaeda carried out suicide attacks against targets in the United States. Two planes were flown into the World Trade Center towers, killing approximately 2,750 people, including more than 400 police officers and firefighters.

Osama bin Laden felt that the Americans were too close to Mecca, violating the holiest place in Islam. This was one of the primary motives for the September 11 attacks.

In May and November of 2003, members of al-Qaeda carried out suicide bombings in Riyadh, Saudi Arabia, which killed both Arabs and Westerners. Muslim religious leaders issued *fatwas*, or religious judgments, stating that suicide attacks and other forms of violence against innocent people are strictly forbidden in Islam.

The death of Osama bin Laden may have hurt al-Qaeda's effectiveness as a terrorist group, but other radical Islamic groups are emerging. Clearly, these groups represent only a small minority of Muslims worldwide. But since the acts of these terrorists make headlines worldwide, some people in the West are uneasy with the culture as a whole.

Princeton University professor and expert on the Middle East Bernard Lewis believes modern Muslims are between a rock and a hard place. "Islam has brought comfort and peace of mind to countless millions of men and women. It has given dignity and meaning to drab and impoverished lives. It has taught people of different races to live in brotherhood and people of different creeds to live side by side in reasonable tolerance. It inspired a great civilization in which others besides Muslims lived creative and useful lives and which, by its achievement, enriched the whole world. But Islam, like other religions, has also known periods when it inspired in some of its followers a mood of hatred and violence. It is our misfortune that part, though by no means all or even most, of the Muslim world is now going through such a period."[2]

Dr. I. Bruce Watson believes the resolution of this Western-Muslim disconnect is possible. "Islam and the West have much to offer each other. Nothing productive will develop while the dominant attitudes are those of suspicion, bigotry, and fear. Islam once played an essential role in preserving knowledge during the ignorance and barbarism of Europe's 'dark ages.' . . . A sympathetic exchange of knowledge, flowing this time from Western societies to Islamic societies, may well . . . permit Islamic societies to enjoy a more creative and significant role in the modern world."[3]

The Taliban

In the early 1990s, a group was formed in Pakistan; it became known as the Taliban. After taking control of Afghanistan in 1996, the Taliban essentially made women non-citizens. Under Taliban laws, women were prohibited from holding a job, were not allowed to attend school, could not leave their homes unless accompanied by a close male relative, and were forced to wear burqas. Some brave women secretly opened schools for girls in private homes, but faced severe punishment if caught. In fact, any woman found breaking the rules could be beaten, flogged, and even executed.

According to the Feminist Majority Foundation advocacy group, a woman who defied Taliban orders by running a home school for girls was killed in front of her family and friends. Another caught trying to escape Afghanistan with a man not related to her was stoned to death for adultery. And an elderly woman had her leg broken by the Taliban

In October 2013, Malala Yousafzai (center right) met with US President Barack Obama (right), his wife Michelle (center left), and his daughter Malia (left). Malala told the president, "If we refocus efforts on education it will make a big impact. There must be greater cooperation between the United States and Pakistan's democratic government starting now. . . . Only then will we ensure lasting peace."[4]

with a metal cable because her ankle was accidentally showing from underneath her *burqa*.[5]

Living conditions for women could be inhumane. Women could not be treated by a male doctor, but no female doctors or nurses were allowed to work. Because of this, women were unable to receive health care and some died.

Eventually, the Taliban was forced out of power and women were once again integrated back into Afghan society. But the Taliban is still pushing to enforce its version of Islamic law in the Middle East. In Pakistan, a teenage girl named Malala Yousafzai was shot by the Taliban in 2012 for speaking out for girls' right to education. After she recovered in a UK hospital, she took her story to the world with her autobiography *I Am Malala*. She has continued to speak out for human rights and was awarded the United Nations Human Rights Prize in 2013.

Cultural Innovators

Shirin Ebadi

 Although not household names in Western countries, these individuals each hold a unique place in Islamic culture, both past and present.

Shirin Ebadi

In 2003, human rights activist Shirin Ebadi became the first Iranian and the first Muslim woman to be awarded the Nobel Peace Prize. She received the award in recognition for her work on behalf of women, children, and refugees. *Forbes* included Ebadi in its 2004 "100 Most Powerful Women in the World" list.

Ebadi has lived in the United Kingdom since 2009 to avoid persecution by Iranian officials over her outspoken criticism of human rights violations.

Muhammad bin Abdul-Wahhab

Muhammad bin Abdul-Wahhab was the scholar responsible for launching the Wahhabi movement of Islam. Although the movement is called Wahhabism in the West, followers consider this name incorrect. They say that Wahhab did not introduce any new ideas, but instead he encouraged a return to the basic principles of Islam. They call their belief system Salafi Islam. Wahhab was born in 1703 in Uyayna, an oasis village in Najd, the central region of Saudi Arabia. It is located about nineteen miles from modern-day Riyadh. His father was a scholar and Wahhab inherited his love of learning. By the time he was ten, he had memorized the Quran. When he was older he went to study in Medina and also traveled to Iraq. In 1740 he returned to Najd, where many people still practiced polytheism.

Upset at the rampant paganism, as well as by Muslims whom he felt were not properly following their faith, Wahhab became a religious activist. He began preaching that there was only one god and he intended to return Islam to what he deemed was its purest form.

Wahhab died in 1792, but Wahhabism eventually became Saudi Arabia's dominant sect of Islam, and is taught in public schools there today. It is a very conservative form of Islam that believes in a literal interpretation of the Quran.

Strict Wahhabis consider anyone who doesn't believe in their form of religion an enemy. Critics say that Wahhabism actually misinterprets Islam and promotes intolerance, encouraging extremists like Osama bin Laden. Although Wahhabism is the dominant sect in Saudi Arabia, it is a minority sect within the whole of Islam.

Zed Al-Refai

Zed Al-Refai is a renowned adventurer and mountain climber. Born in Kuwait on October 28, 1966, Al-Refai was educated in Finland as a youth, then earned his Bachelor's Degree in Political Science in the United States. During school breaks he traveled across the United States, exploring the Rockies and other regions.

Al-Refai moved to Switzerland in 1992 and began mountain climbing there. A few years later, he took a vacation to Nepal where he became entranced by Mt. Everest in the Himalayas. He decided he wanted to try to climb the mountain. After training for

Zed Al-Refai is shown here at Aconcagua in Argentina. When he climbed this mountain in 2004, he became the first Arab to climb the "Seven Summits," the highest peaks on each of the seven continents.

several years climbing smaller peaks, in 1999 Al-Refai became the first Arab to summit Mt. McKinley, the highest peak in North America. He failed at his first attempt to climb Mt. Everest when he became ill due to the effects of the low oxygen levels at high elevations. He was successful the second time around, though, and became the first Arab to climb this mountain in 2003. He took the challenge further when he became the first Arab to scale the highest summit on each of the seven continents, which besides McKinley and Everest includes: Carstenz Pyramid in Oceania; Elbrus in Europe; Kilimanjaro in Africa; Vinson Massif in Antarctica; and Aconcagua in South America.

Al-Refai is the president of the Arabian Mountaineering and Alpine Climbing Club, which he founded to share his love for mountain climbing with people in the Middle East. He shares, "[Mountain climbing] is exciting because you deal with elements that are beyond human reach. You don't know what to expect next, so it is all about living the moment and finding one's self. Challenging your own abilities, rather than challenging the mountain."[1] He is also a coffee merchant and has homes in both Switzerland and the United Arab Emirates.

Nimah Nawwab

Born in Malaysia to a Meccan family, Nimah Nawwab is an internationally acclaimed literary figure. Nawwab, who graduated

Nimah Nawwab (pictured here with film director Hamzah Jamjoom) says her influences include thirteenth-century Persian poet Jalaluddin Rumi and eighth-century Muslim Saint Rabia Basri.

from college with a Bachelor of Arts in English Literature, aims to increase tolerance among people worldwide. She speaks at conferences and presentations to encourage this acceptance. She also teaches workshops for aspiring teen and adult writers and poets.

Nawwab's articles and essays about Saudi society, customs, and Islam have been published throughout the Middle East and in Western publications as well. Her book of poetry, *The Unfurling*, speaks about issues that Muslim men and women face throughout the world, but especially the Arab world. The poems feature strong themes of freedom, family, culture, faith, tradition, and tolerance. She currently lives in Dhahran, Saudi Arabia, with her family.

Majid Majidi

Majid Majidi is an internationally-acclaimed Iranian film director, film producer, and screenwriter. His film *Children of Heaven* was nominated for the Academy Award for Best Foreign Language Film in 1998.

Born April 17, 1959, to a middle-class family in Tehran, Majidi joined amateur theater groups as a teenager. After high school, he studied art at the Institute of Dramatic Art in Tehran. He appeared in numerous movies before he started writing and directing short films. His feature film directing debut *Baduk* won awards for Best New Film and Best Screen Play at Tehran's Fajr Film Festival in 1992. His 1999 film, *The Color of Paradise*, won the Best Picture award at the Montreal International Film Festival.

In 2013 Majidi finished filming a movie about the life of young Muhammad. Although the movie does not show Muhammad's face, it reignited the question of whether any depiction of the prophet is acceptable. Majidi's next film, *Floating Gardens*, is based in India and is due out in 2015.

Majid Majidi says he was artistic even as a child. "At the age of twelve, I acted in my first play. I enjoyed theater and acting, so I continued. Later, I was given the opportunity to direct. So I did. From that I wrote and developed my first film. That, of course, was my most difficult project. But a filmmaker's first film is in many ways his most defining work. Even though there are many obstacles, there is still no excuse to create a weak piece."[2]

Experiencing Islamic Culture in the United States

If you want to know more about Middle Eastern Islamic culture, you may be able to experience it right in your own neighborhood! Most mosques in the United States welcome visitors of any religion, so you might like to attend if you are interested in knowing more about the Islamic faith. You can visit restaurants that feature Middle Eastern style cuisine, and you can also find live shows, movies, and museum exhibits that highlight Middle Eastern culture. Here are some resources to get started:

> Salatomatic: An online guide to finding mosques, Middle Eastern restaurants, and Islamic schools. http://www.salatomatic.com/
> Yelp: Search for "Middle Eastern" near you for restaurants and cultural events. http://www.yelp.com/

Try your hand at Middle Eastern cooking with these recipe resources. (Be sure you have adult supervision when working in the kitchen!)
> AllRecipes.com: Middle Eastern Recipes
> http://allrecipes.com/recipes/world-cuisine/middle-eastern/
> Khalife, Maria. *The Middle Eastern Cookbook*. Northampton, MA: Interlink, 2007.
> Saveur: Middle Eastern Cuisine
> http://www.saveur.com/cuisine/middle-eastern

There are many Middle Eastern films that are available in the United States. Check out the international section of your local DVD store, or look for one of these films:
> *Blackboards*. Directed by Samira Makhmalbaf, 2002.
> *Children of Heaven*. Directed by Majid Majidi, 2007.
> *The Color of Paradise*. Directed by Majid Majidi, 2000.

Purchase digital music or attend a concert. Start by listening to Middle Eastern radio:
> SoundCloud: Radio Middle East FM
> https://soundcloud.com/arabamericanvision
> TuneIn: Middle Eastern Music Radio
> http://tunein.com/radio/Middle-Eastern-Music-g155/

Map of the Middle East

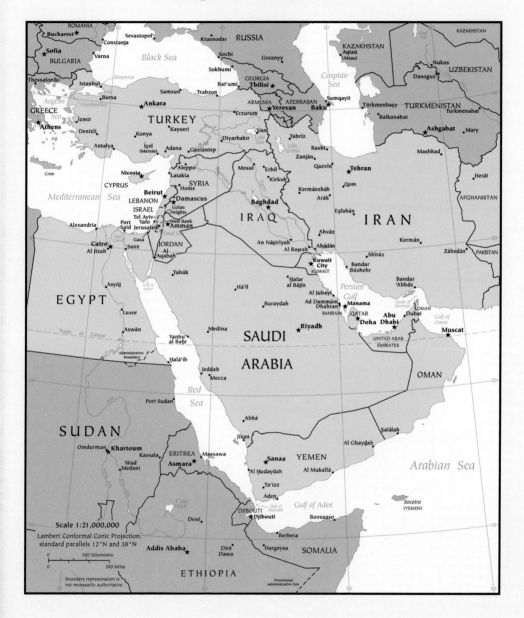

TIMELINE

570	Birth of Muhammad.
622	The hijra, Muhammad flees to Medina.
630	Muslims capture Mecca.
642	Egypt becomes part of the Islamic Empire.
711	Muslim armies invade Spain.
1100s	Christian Crusaders invade Egypt.
1400s	Saud Dynasty founded in the region around modern-day Riyadh.
1526	The Islamic Mughal Empire rules India.
1703	Birth of Muhammad bin Abdul-Wahhab.
1803	Mecca is conquered by the Wahhabis.
1933	Kingdom of Saudi Arabia is founded.
1996	The Taliban takes control of Afghanistan.
1998	Majid Majidi's film *Children of Heaven* is nominated for the Academy Award for Best Foreign Language Film.
2003	Zed Al-Refai becomes the first Arab to climb Mt. Everest.
2004	Iranian human rights activist Shirin Ebadi is listed on the *Forbes* "100 Most Powerful Women in the World" list.
2010	The Arab Spring begins with anti-government protests in Tunisia and Algeria.
2012	Pakistani teenager Malala Yousafzai is shot by the Taliban after speaking out for girls' right to education.
2014	The Sharjah emirate of the United Arab Emirates is named the Capital of Islamic Culture for the year.

Arab Spring protests in Cairo, Egypt

CHAPTER NOTES

Chapter 1. Conquest of Mecca
1. Ishaq, *The Life of Muhammad*, trans. A. Guillaume (New York: Oxford University Press, 1955), p. 118.
2. Ira M. Lapidus, *A History of Islamic Societies* (Cambridge, UK: Cambridge University Press, 1988), p. 27.
3. Flemming Rose, *Washington Post*, "Why I Published Those Cartoons," February 19, 2006. http://www.washingtonpost.com/wp-dyn/content/article/2006/02/17/AR2006021702499.html
4. Paul Richard, *Washington Post*, "In Art Museums, Portraits Illuminate a Religious Taboo," February 14, 2006.
5. Ibid.
6. Eric Weiner, NPR, *Analysis*, "Why Cartoons of the Prophet Insult Muslims," February 8, 2006.

Chapter 2. Evolution of Islamic Culture
1. M. Florian, *The Moors in Spain*, The Werner Company, 1910. Heritage History. http://www.heritage-history.com/?c=read&author=florian&book=moors&story=_front

Chapter 3. Muslim Religious Traditions
1. Pew Research Center, "Mapping the Global Muslim Population," October 7, 2009. http://www.pewforum.org/2009/10/07/mapping-the-global-muslim-population/

Chapter 4. Islamic Social Customs
1. Mark Long, AP News Service, "Crowd Roars for First Saudi Woman in Olympics," August 8, 2012. http://www.komonews.com/sports/Crowd-roars-for-first-Saudi-woman-Sarah-Attar-in-Olympics-165453446.html

Chapter 5. Arts and Science
1. Mawlana Sikander Khan Pathan, Furqaan Institute of Quranic Healing, "Every Illness Has a Cure: The Islamic Perspective," April 8, 2009. http://www.fiqh.org/2009/04/every-illness-has-a-cure-the-islamic-perspective/

2. Emilie Savage-Smith, National Institutes of Health, "Medieval Islamic Medicine," *Islamic Culture and the Medical Arts*, September 12, 1994. http://www.nlm.nih.gov/exhibition/islamic_medical/islamic_02.html
3. David Stipp, *Scientific American*, "How Intermittent Fasting Might Help You Live a Longer and Healthier Life," January 2013. http://www.scientificamerican.com/article.cfm?id=how-intermittent-fasting-might-help-you-live-longer-healthier-life

Chapter 6. Politics and World View
1. Academy of Achievement, "Norman Schwarzkopf Interview," June 26, 1992. http://www.achievement.org/autodoc/page/sch0int-4
2. Bernard Lewis, *Atlantic*, "The Roots of Muslim Rage," September 1990. http://www.theatlantic.com/doc/prem/199009/muslim-rage
3. Dr. I. Bruce Watson, *Insight*, "Islam and its Challenges in the Modern World," vol. 12, issue 1 May 1997.
4. CNN, "Malala to Obama: Drone Strikes 'Fueling Terrorism,'" October 12, 2013. http://www.cnn.com/2013/10/12/politics/obamas-meet-malalas/index.html
5. Feminist Majority Foundation, "Campaign for Afghan Women and Girls." http://www.feminist.org/afghan/taliban_women.asp

Chapter 7. Cultural Innovators
1. EverestNews.com, "One on One Interview with Everest Summiter Zed Al Refai," August 26, 2005. http://www.everestnews.com/stories2005/zed08262005.htm
2. Ross Anthony, Hollywood Report Card, "Children of Heaven—the Interview." http://rossanthony.com/interviews/majidi.shtml

FURTHER READING

Books

1001 Inventions & Awesome Facts from Muslim Civilization. Washington, DC: National Geographic, 2012.

Khan, Rukhsana. *Muslim Child: A Collection of Short Stories and Poems.* Toronto, ON: Napoleon Publishing, 1999.

Yousafzai, Malala. *I Am Malala.* New York: Little, Brown, and Company, 2013.

On the Internet

Muslim Kids TV: Videos and Crafts for Muslim Children
    http://www.muslimkidstv.com/
PBS: "Global Connections, The Middle East"
    http://www.pbs.org/wgbh/globalconnections/mideast/questions/women/
PBS: *Islam, Empire of Faith,* "Art"
    http://www.pbs.org/empires/islam/cultureart.html
World Religions for Kids: "Islam"
    https://sites.google.com/site/worldreligionsforkids/islam

Works Consulted

Academy of Achievement. "Norman Schwarzkopf Interview." June 26, 1992.
    http://www.achievement.org/autodoc/page/sch0int-4
Anthony, Ross. "Children of Heaven—the Interview." Hollywood Report Card.
    http://rossanthony.com/interviews/majidi.shtml
CNN. "Malala to Obama: Drone Strikes 'Fueling Terrorism.'" October 12, 2013.
    http://www.cnn.com/2013/10/12/politics/obamas-meet-malalas/index.html
EverestNews.com. "One on One Interview with Everest Summiter Zed Al Refai."
    August 26, 2005. http://www.everestnews.com/stories2005/zed08262005.htm
Feldman, Noah. "Why Shariah?" *New York Times,* March 16, 2008.
    http://www.nytimes.com/2008/03/16/magazine/16Shariah-t.
    html?pagewanted=all&_r=0
Feminist Majority Foundation. "Campaign for Afghan Women and Girls."
    http://www.feminist.org/afghan/taliban_women.asp
First Arab to Summit Mount Everest. "Born to Summit."
    http://www.foreverest.com/portfolio.php
Florian, M. *The Moors in Spain.* The Werner Company, 1910. Heritage History.
    http://www.heritage-history.com/?c=read&author=florian&book=moors
    &story=_fro.
Hitti, Philip K. *History of the Arabs: From the Earliest Times to the Present.* New York:
    Macmillan, 1951.
Hunter, Shireen T., editor. *The Politics of Islamic Revivalism: Diversity and Unity.*
    Bloomington, IN: Indiana University Press, 1988.
Ishaq. *The Life of Muhammad.* Translated by A. Guillaume. New York: Oxford
    University Press, 1955.
Islamic Medical Association of North America. "Information for Health Care
    Providers When Dealing with a Muslim Patient." http://c.ymcdn.com/sites/
    www.imana.org/resource/resmgr/Files/ethics_4.pdf
Johnson, Toni, and Lauren Vriens. "Islam: Governing under Sharia." Council on
    Foreign Relations, January 9, 2013. http://www.cfr.org/religion/islam-
    governing-under-sharia/p8034

FURTHER READING

Lapidus, Ira M. *A History of Islamic Societies.* Cambridge, UK: Cambridge University Press, 1988.

Lewis, Bernard. "The Roots of Muslim Rage." *Atlantic*, September 1990. http://www.theatlantic.com/doc/prem/199009/muslim-rage

Long, Mark. "Crowd Roars for First Saudi Woman in Olympics." AP News Service, August 8, 2012. http://www.komonews.com/sports/Crowd-roars-for-first-Saudi-woman-Sarah-Attar-in-Olympics-165453446.html

Nimah J. Nawwab: Writer, Poet, Photographer, Activist. http://www.nimahnawwab.com/home.html

Pathan, Mawlana Sikander Khan. "Every Illness Has a Cure: The Islamic Perspective." Furqaan Institute of Quranic Healing, April 8, 2009. http://www.fiqh.org/2009/04/every-illness-has-a-cure-the-islamic-perspective/

PBS. "Analysis: Wahhabism." *Frontline.* http://www.pbs.org/wgbh/pages/frontline/shows/saudi/analyses/wahhabism.html

PBS. "Muhammad." *Islam: Empire of Faith.* http://www.pbs.org/empires/islam/profilesmuhammed.html

Pew Research Center. "Mapping the Global Muslim Population." October 7, 2009. http://www.pewforum.org/2009/10/07/mapping-the-global-muslim-population/

Reeves, Philip. "Malala, Hailed Around the World, Controversial at Home." NPR, December 10, 2013.

Richard, Paul. "In Art Museums, Portraits Illuminate a Religious Taboo." *Washington Post*, February 14, 2006.

Roebuck, Carl. *The World of Ancient Times.* New York: Charles Scribner's Sons, 1966.

Rose, Flemming. "Why I Published Those Cartoons." *Washington Post*, February 19, 2006. http://www.washingtonpost.com/wp-dyn/content/article/2006/02/17/AR2006021702499.html

Savage-Smith, Emilie. "Medieval Islamic Medicine." *Islamic Culture and the Medical Arts.* National Institutes of Health, September 12, 1994. http://www.nlm.nih.gov/exhibition/islamic_medical/islamic_02.html

Srivastava, Priyanka. "Iranian Legend Majidi Will Shoot New Film Floating Gardens in India." Daily Mail Online India, September 11, 2013. http://www.dailymail.co.uk/indiahome/indianews/article-2417895/Iranian-legend-Majidi-shoot-new-film-Floating-Gardens-India.html

Stipp, David. "How Intermittent Fasting Might Help You Live a Longer and Healthier Life." *Scientific American*, January 2013. http://www.scientificamerican.com/article.cfm?id=how-intermittent-fasting-might-help-you-live-longer-healthier-life

Watson, Dr. I. Bruce. "Islam and its Challenges in the Modern World." *Insight*, vol. 12, issue 1, May 1997.

Weiner, Eric. "Why Cartoons of the Prophet Insult Muslims." NPR, *Analysis*, February 8, 2006.

GLOSSARY

Allah (uh-LAH)—The Arabic name for God.

allies (AL-ahyz)—Groups or nations that agree to cooperate with each other for a common purpose.

amnesty (AM-nuh-stee)—Official forgiveness of a crime.

caliph (KEY-lif)—A Muslim leader who succeeded Muhammad.

contemporaneous (kuhn-tem-puh-REY-nee-uhs)—taking place in the same time period.

deity (DEE-ih-tee)—A god or goddess.

hadith (hah-DEETH)—The deeds and sayings of Muhammad.

Hajj (HAJ)—the annual Muslim pilgrimage to Mecca.

holistic (hoh-LIS-tik)—Considering all the components of a person including mind, body, and soul.

idol (AHYD-uhl)—An image or object that is worshipped religiously.

imam (ih-MAHM)—Arabic word for leader generally applied to religious leaders.

irrigation (ir-ih-GEY-shuhn)—The process of watering land to grow crops.

jihad (ji-HAHD)—A holy war against non-believers; Arabic word meaning "to struggle."

mosque (MAWSK)—A Muslim place of public worship.

nomadic (noh-MAD-ik)—Living without any permanent home.

oasis (oh-EY-sis)—A small area within a desert that has plants and a water source (plural: oases).

pagan (PEY-guhn)—Related to a polytheistic religion.

piety (PAHY-ih-tee)—Devotion to God and the practices prescribed by God.

pilgrimage (PIL-gruh-mij)—A journey to a sacred place.

polytheism (pol-ee-THEE-iz-uhm)—Belief in more than one god.

prophet (PROF-it)—A person who can receive messages from God and pass those messages onto the people.

satirical (suh-TIR-ih-kuhl)—Ironic, sarcastic, making fun of.

sect (SEKT)—A subgroup or denomination of a religious, political, or philosophical belief system.

secular (SEK-yuh-ler)—Related to the non-religious world.

sedentary (SED-uhn-ter-ee)—Living in one place, not moving regularly.

souk (SOOK)—An Arab market.

tenet (TEN-it)—A main principle or belief of a group or religion.

transcend (tran-SEND)—To go beyond or exceed.

umma (UHM-uh)—The worldwide community of Muslims.

INDEX

About the Author

Kathleen Tracy has been a journalist and author for more than twenty years. She has traveled extensively throughout her career, traveling throughout Europe, the South Pacific, and Central America. The author also lived in North Africa for two months while researching an article on movie production, spending extensive time in Tunisia and Egypt.